A Moment's Notice

A collection of poems

by

Michael Sands

A Moment's Notice

A collection of poems
by

Michael Sands

Clachan Publishing
3 Drumavoley Park, Ballycastle, BT54 6PE,
Glens of Antrim.

First published 2015

Email: info@clachanpublishing.com
Website: http://clachanpublishing-com.

This book is sold under the condition that it is not sold,
by way of trade or otherwise, be lent, resold, hired out or in otherwise
circulated without the publisher's prior consent in any form
of binding or cover other than that in which it is published and
without similar condition, including this condition, being imposed on the
subsequent purchaser.

Clachan Publishing, Ballycastle. The Glens of Antrim.
http://www.clachanpublishing.com

For
Catherine, Katie and Tóla.

Barry Kerr - musician, artist, singer and songwriter.

In Ireland today we are only a few generations removed from a bardic tradition. A tradition of poetry, story and song which flowed through antiquity unbroken until recent times. Some may dispute that this tradition was lost forever with the last of the Gaelic poets, the likes of Séamas Dall Mac Cuarta, Art Mac Cumhaigh of the Fews and Peadar Ó Doirnín, I would argue to the contrary. Here in the writings of Michael Sands I see a continuation of this bardic tradition, a connection with what went before and what is to come, working with words is in his very DNA. I feel a vitality and sense of place in the work, vocabulary and metre portraying the familiar yet somehow all the while evoking the mystical and veiled. Michael's work opens a window to the spirit, to the depth of what it is to be Irish in the 21st century. His words show pedigree and provenance, a consciousness of roots and what he has inherited from our tradition, a continuance of legacy for which the Irish people are famed.

Mickey McConnell - writer, singer/song writer & poet

In days like these, in times like these how badly we need those of courage to carry the tattered flag of understanding into the battleground. I salute you and celebrate what you write. Nothing more needs to be said.

Jason O'Rourke - writer and musician

This collection, Michael's second, is rooted in his environment: family, society, music, the natural world outside his window. The poems keenly observe the everyday, drawing our attention to its finer details, which are presented to us with fondness and irreverent mirth. Michael's poetry at times sparkles with wit and clever rhymes, and at others it is earnest in its tenderness and humanity. Underlying the verse is an encompassing love for his world and its people – turn the page, and step inside.

Contents

Contents	i
Foreword	iii
Breathing	1
More than One	2
Garden	3
Man with Pram	4
Bodhrán	6
Concertina	7
Fiddle	8
March	10
As it was Left	11
Day Breaking	12
Interview	14
Suddenly	16
Sticks	17
Road	18
Teach an Cheoil (The Music House)	20
Accordion	21
Christmas (Beli)Eve	22
Doors	23
Not Fade Away	25
Missing in Action	27
No Offence	28
Playing Dead	30
Play Ground	31
Thunder and Lightning	32
Evening in September	33
Daylight Saving	34
Getting like Thunder	35
Finger Chase	36
Flute	37
Guitar	39
Novices	40
Tenor Banjo	41
The Other Mountain	42
Bird Song?	44
Away Day	45

Shadow	47
Picture Book	48
The Half House	49
Curtains	50
Suit	51
Enough	52
Jetsam	53
The Troubles	54
Trams	56
As the Crow Flies	57
Upon a Laneway Late	58
Ór (Gold)	60
Big Bike	61
Splash	62
Name	63
The Hunt for the Rat - A True Story	64

Foreword

In his earlier collection of poems I interpreted Michael Sands' work as a wandering, a journey of adventure, of discovery from his native South Down, moving northward to eventually settle close to the Antrim Coast in the presence of Fair Head. As the settling follows the journey, I began to move through his new collection with this understanding in mind, and very quickly realised what was happening - something I had been waiting on for many years - as I come from a similar traditional music and song background as Michael, though a generation older. It came in full flow in the poems, a new growth, a new blossom and bloom on ancient ways and rituals, a freshening of traditional things, a youthful presence moving in on old and venerable art. It was there in abundance, poem after poem, preserving by rejuvenating, a spring breeze on the features of things.

I was particularly moved by the way he revealed hitherto unidentified personalities regarding the musical instruments - the bodhrán, the fiddle, accordion, banjo, and so on, that out of his travels he found and gave fresh life to many roots when he returned. The experience of learning Irish in relation to a reinterpretation of the landscape and surroundings was simply superb.

But it is not just these elements of rural artistic life that he addresses, dear as they are to him. In keeping with the poet's natural dynamic, all things interest him in the wider social and cultural domain.

Key to everything in this collection is a truly genuine poetic faculty, a sensitivity to his surroundings in every respect, a devotion to his art, and one constantly in touch with the flow and flux of things as "A Moment's Notice" signifies. But the actual "Moment's Notice" on its own is just one part of the poet's armoury. It is the merely the moment of inspiration, a fleeting thing that will vanish unless captured and held and preserved through the writer's powers of construction. Form is central, and Michael's major strength is his insistence throughout on form and structure in order to give life to the inspiration. There is consistent beauty and originality of expression in these poems, that a natural muse is being worked on relentlessly, a natural gift constantly seeking perfection.

In this collection as I see it, Michael Sands has done a lofty service to his inheritance by releasing an overall fresh growth, fresh flowering on many profound ways and aspirations of the people. This, after all, is the poet's specific responsibility and he has been faithful to it. He has also, through his overall work and this collection in particular, given his native South Down one of its finest ever affirmations of poetic art.

DAY BREAKING

The mists of morning melt
slowly into light,
and I am invaded
by another day.

Peter Makem – author, writer and poet.

acknowledgements

Thanks are due to:

Patricia Hutton for the use of her photograph on the front cover.
Tom Mervyn for the use of his photograph on the back cover.
Paul Eliasberg for the use of his photograph in the poem "Suit".

You know my method. It is founded upon the observation of trifles.
    Sherlock Holmes,

        Arthur Conan Doyle, *The Bascombe Valley Mystery,*

breathing

For Cóla
Bone fingered hail raps hard the window
urged by north wind, chaos willing.
Winter whispers scream and test and show
the value of sealed panes. The air's chilling

and we look to black iron as conduction
heats the hearth and heart. Our young lad
shivers (bug going round). The reduction
from himself is unfair, remedy will be had.

Silent as his bed time passes. Moments
in defiance of his room I have not noticed.
Gently he fills my lap, shortly whence
we breath together. Unity I've also missed.

I can face any gale, or storm or mountain peak,
or snow bound road or over flowing stream
for I am filled by him. Bravery need not seek,
nor courage, I have more than they would dream.

Our chests move together briefly, 'til he leaves
my longer inhalations with busier ones.
I'll carry him up. He's sound asleep and believes
in me, in us. What strength daughters and sons…

More Than One

For Catherine

It's hardly fair to say you're the one, it's not enough.
Nor is it right to limit you so. You wear many faces

and fulfil a legion roles in pursuit of all the stuff
of day to day, the to-ing and fro-ing between places.

The you of so many Thursdays ago, I see her still
in moments at the slowing of the sun or in a secret smile.

Though she was ushered from the stage, off the windowsill,
the you of our new house bowed, in such energetic style.

She fixed up, made ready and prepared the special room.
The room with cot and soft edges where a daughter slept

under a new mother's gaze. Every tear or moment's gloom
relieved and chased away. Every promise so solemnly kept

to guide her, and I, into a homecoming. A return to the vast
open spaces of childhood, where the fields have names.

The surroundings freed you of stuck slow cars in fast
lanes, cramped streets with no room for children's games.

I watched you meet your younger self in passing and since
then another you. The you of growing children, chasing

a minute's calm. In its scarcity we strive to convince
ourselves to keep on. But we do and do so facing

into whatever obstacles. And having weathered
many storms we hold fast. Whatever more we do

we'll meet life along our path like some boat tethered
on a lake. I'll touch the water and sail with all of you.

Garden

For Mary

I am lucky to have patience for certain things, understanding
for others. I will select less physical pastimes, undemanding
on the back. She has no such tendencies and no qualms
whatever about lifting, pushing or pulling. Her palms

grasp and tug at weeds, old branches or stones that need shoving.
The spade manifests thoughts to clear paths or lovingly
make room for heathers. There is obvious determination
to alleviate the eye from concrete and observe the celebration

of colour. It can be a triumph to raise myself from bed
on certain mornings. She raises beds and inters, instead
of fatigue, new life. Her soil accomplice will cling
to clothes and under nails to remind us that everything

is contact. These skills do not however grow on trees.
They are harvested from the stooped backs and bent knees
of previous crops. From land wise parents who, more
than we know, relied on bees, on green shoots long before

plastic food. I see them revel in well behaved weather,
three generations of being outside. A mother together
with daughter's daughters cultivating a family yield
as ever younger seedlings scuttle about from field

to field. My contribution is restricted to mechanised
cuttings, exasperated hammer swings. They're not surprised
as the chaff and rough of curse words take to the air.
I'm happy enough to learn and watch them growing there.

Man with Pram

Is there a more unsettling sight
as he trundles behind, no power yet might
any moment beat hard his chest
to satisfy the inner, testosteroned test
that was the call of the beast of his day?

Is he the zenith of humanity's wit?
At such times you would not believe it.
His hard hands grip soft padded handles
instead of spears, rocks, stag fatted candles
and he walks the four tyre tracked way.

He evolved as king from history's plains
and now all he has to show for his pains
is this non-effort push and then avoid
arms, legs and crowds in town all devoid
of challenge and chase, his shoulders droop.

Ousted from his throne of ancestral tribes
to someplace beneath the vociferous vibes
of his charge. The little creature plastic protected
with wipes and creams and all such connected
stuff to sort the foulest of soup!

The prams themselves like banquets of yore
with interior heating, TVs and more
for fear the passenger may want for two seconds…
Woe, far from the chariots of Rome now he reckons
this vehicle he so solemnly steers.

Bad enough on the street but oh shopping aisles
that simply go on for miles upon miles
where his meek manoeuvres are scorned as like magic
the wee one bounds out. Now empty and tragic
his pram is empty! Realised, his worst fears.

But this is the way, the old ways have ended.
The days of her pushing? What nature intended?
'Til nature he realised, herself is a mother
and is changing the rules from those to another,
he may get used and well used to the task.

So the bane of all men call it buggy or pram
is here to stay and will ignore any qualm
like pride or street cred and all such excuses
for she has discovered that a man has more uses
and to deny it he'd better not ask!

bodhrán

For Comaí Taylor

Handled wood, stretched tight thereon
goat skin, cured. In time resurrected.
It is life after death. After night, dawn,
the echo of man and soil reconnected.

Tapped tacks, beyond sight's horizons
disappear past equators and secure
rhythm. They fast hold liaisons
'twixt bars and beats, simple and pure.

Not all for the cross. There is new faith
in deeper rims. The laying on of hands
that push, explore and lean on grace
notes leading on to promised lands.

Without words it speaks. Refined sound,
denied in design such musical quotes.
Supportive of tune like some tilled ground
is for the sowing of all the wild oats.

It's partner, the cipín, a willing quill
of emotion. The ink of expression
its touch. Light, heavy, furious or still
in masterful grip backbone to the session.

Its circumference a nation, enraptured.
Basic antiquity, passion unmatched,
tempo distilled, breath and heart captured...
Bodhrán play on, no strings attached

Concertina

for Jason O'Rourke

Hand held at arms' length, strapped in
and grip secured, ready to begin.
He inhales and draws air over reeds
and into himself. The tune needs

freedom. He acquiesces with unity
as if conjuring light from darkness he
presses hexagons. Twelve degrees
of precision that only fingertips see.

In their midst, bellows, controlled
in centimetres and inches, times six fold.
But these notes are not of the sea
or shanty. They are Ireland, jig and reel

hornpipe, polka and lament. What joy!
What gift of energy, in the employ
of experts whose influence from Clare
and Belfast, enthuses all. Mastery of air.

It lives among the peaks, the range
of crotchets composers might arrange
in the higher lines of staves allegrezza.
Their harvest is as good as it gets

and the room is held tight between
breaths. The origin almost unseen
atop his lap, hot amongst the embers
of music the hearing heart remembers.

In the end he'll draw the last tone
and caress nickel silver. In its box alone
it rests. You'd hardly credit at all
tempests, tapped from a source so small.

Fiddle

For Paul Flynn

I marvel at its vast and minute range,
this wooden gold beyond all measure.
What banquets deemed to arrange,
what céilís, honouring the treasure

in the ebbing and flow of a fiddle.
Such complex identity, what bravado
to cross the barriers that often riddle
and confine those unwilling. We owe

the finesse and skill of its players
smoothing horse hair across seasons.
They covet perfection, like night prayers
who bargain desires against reasons.

The scroll, such extravagant geometry,
spiralling atop four string pegs
whose scalpel accuracy, dark symmetry
hearts twist and stir dancers' legs.

The neck, child delicate, easy held
and ever designed for palm and thumb.
Its touch, like skin or some other meld
of bone and time, of whisper and hum.

The gouged shore of its body, indented
by musical wind and constant tide.
The curvature of horizons invented
emotions to induce that none may hide

the clarity of its beating heart.
Its tail piece and 'f' holes ornately
await the long visitor who will impart
friction and melodies, common and stately.

But not a sound 'til the bridge is crossed.
And to the Devil those who doubt
the task. For many souls are surely lost,
in regret and in rosin to limp about.

And finally the bow, that sculpted key.
In such hands that it would turn
and unlock brightness for worlds to see
making the ears of its listeners burn.

March

Before the fires of May you come
before the April Fool
though not quick enough for some
are your mornings crisp and cool.

Two sides of a warring coin,
the first half and the second
as cold and heat in battle join
the factions there are beckoned.

Winter waits in sombre mood
and holds the earth so tight
that not a blade of grass that stood
is scar free from the fight.

The mountain tops sit white and clean
and would the year around
on orders choke the growing green
and freeze the waking ground.

March you hold the world in wait
'til eyes heavy slowly see
that Spring has not abandoned fate
to wrestle Winter free.

To melt her icy finger nails
from tree and hedge and soul
and make a warmer place for snails
and bird and bush and mole.

Slower than a time piece tick
the battle surely turns
as starting slow but ending quick
Spring from earth the Winter burns.

The new free peaks begin to stretch,
the trees bid all good day.
Such scenes on my mind do etch
that March has had its say.

as it was left

She scans the kitchen for the out of place;
for items in defiance of contempt
and order. She then checks her face,
her collar and hair (being unkempt

meant trouble growing up). She negates
these thoughts and smiles at perfection
in a mirror, wall bound. Breakfast plates
though are cause for exception.

Each morning the crumbed remains
of toast, hints of butter, a rub of jam
do not receive sentence. Tea stains
slow soak into wood like salt into ham.

The spreading knife, steel strewn,
lies at lazy angles and its jagged edges
await challenge. A clock glance and soon
she is high wire walking the ledges

of life and loss. Time tantalises.
Tea break chat, dinner orders and such,
a prelude to a door opening. She fantasises
something askew. It is all too much.

Her steps quicken over familiar kerbstones
until breath heavy she turns a key. Bereft
of patience she sees…and subtly groans.
All is unchanged, exactly as it was left.

Day breaking

The mists of morning melt
slowly into light
and I am invaded
by another day.
The clock hands
have broken my fight
and my tie ensures
that's how I stay…

No song to sing.

My ironed shirt behind
the door awaits
my unerring call
at five to nine.
I'll trouser up
then close the gates
and from nine to five
feel far from fine…

A fake gold ring.

The qwerty keyboard taps
of mouse and man
a shouting silence
amongst the staff.
The banality of tea.
A blowing fan
the rustle of paper
A distant laugh…

A door's in-swing.

My time is duly lost
in this daily chore
of empty words
and worthless prose.
At the bank's altar
I must adore,
a grotesque gigolo
Yes, I do suppose…

I'm a broken thing.

But broken or not
I must attend
and barter myself
to such a task.
This twisted affair
pulls at my heart.
Needs without end
is it too much to ask…

This money to bring.

Interview

We surveyed each other over the desk, our silent border.
I wondered as to my tie's straightness. Did I look ok?

Enough at least to begin, to adhere to the natural order
of things. His colleague made a pen loud note and turned away.

I wrapped my feet around the legs of the chair, out of sight.
There was a comfort in it. I pondered the water on offer

but did not bother pouring it in this self made plight.
I remembered how much I hated ties. Should I proffer

a banality? The weather perhaps? Or other inconsequence?
No. He leaned forward with his belly behind his shoes

and asked the first question. He'd asked it to all in sequence
and there was no life in it. It was general, no personal views

required. I balanced a selection of replies for a second or two.
Do I play the game and yield to the greyness of the ritual?

I could say how I'd fulfil all requirements. How I could do
an excellent job within the team and garner some mutual

respect. I looked into his eyes at that point and realised
wit would be a wondrous loss on him. Humour would

disappear into the black hole of his forced lack of surprise.
I exhaled a resigned breath. I would do the best I could.

This was a mistake and yet an affirmation. I was not
cut for this cloth. At heart I am a hippy, a ne'er do well

in this exacting world. The moments thereafter sought
out any hiding place. I so desperately wanted to tell

him to 'fu*k off'. I resisted and pushed back the chair.
We knew the end had come, no reason to remain.

With all alacrity and twist the tie was thrown into the air
and I was free. Free to redeem the trial in some poetic vein.

Suddenly

Roast chicken on a plate, takes me to some date
I cannot quite recall
But never far behind replaying thoughts remind
me of her, standing tall.

Guinness with its luscious cream, and as in a dream
we are in Dublin town.
No more pleasing sight from an extraordinary night
than her settling darkness down.

'Salt n' Shake', the ancient snack takes me further back
to Lurgan. I was six.
She said "Offer **all** within. Please, do not begin
to grip." So much for childish tricks!

As I drive the motorway, Belfast does quietly say
"The children's ward,
paintings tall and bright." I saw them every night
and life was my reward.

That type of car, big and wide, all of us inside
heading south late somewhere.
O'Connell Street stretched for years, us in laughing tears
behind. Delighted just being there.

Upon a lane a well used tyre, rolling fast from higher
ground. Stay between the hedges.
A branch that holds a piece of rope. We did surely cope
with trapeze grips and wooden edges.

Your first bright, constant smile, clearly it did me beguile
in a Thursday Newry bar.
I see it still, musician sewn, who could have ever known
It would take us where we are.

Sticks

She had a keen eye, like a cockler, sandy fingered,
and where flame warmed her stove, soot lingered.

In stones I found more potential and eyeing a crow
I'd plan its doom. But it's cold and I must follow

her zipped, soft ankle boots with fur peeping over.
Her footsteps lean gently on the fine gravel cover

that ices the yard. She bends for Elm stragglers,
half a foot, like witches wands bent and ragged.

She has enough, ten say, with leaves on a few
clinging on gamely. I'm the height of her skirt, blue

and plain. She surveys doors, turns a silver wheel
then tugs a lever. The tray is fine. She begins to feel

around for the Newry Reporter. "Your job," she says.
I crinkle deaths and marriages, ads and sporting days,

pictures of armoured cars and accounts of court cases,
a furnace judgement for all. Top hats, clean faces

and singers unaware of how their music travels.
Then the sticks, placed before my work unravels.

A red match scratches over a rough runway
and is the start of it. I smell the sticks to this day,

the sense of outside, the birth of fire, mumbling
and as the cracks come the spells come tumbling…

Later I'll say, "Fetch me those sticks there…"
We shall collect our own kindling and think of her.

Road

I met myself coming home.
At least, that's how it felt.
The Ryan Road leads to some
other world and I melt

into hedges and gates, cattle
and adventure. Hoof holes
trip me. My bones rattle
and only after many rolls

do I stop. I remember that.
I echo in fields, behind walls
where nettles lurk near flat
stones and thistles. Calls

come loud in moonlight.
I'm approaching new choices.
Crossan? One winter's night
we walked it to mass. Voices

now whins and ragweeds.
I turn left, away under leaves
on a Desert Road. Swings and deeds
of youth. They are tying sheaves

and us running after, a distraction.
Protestant land offers Benagh,
right and downhill. The traction
of tyre and time, the subtle claw

of age, pull me toward Glenvale
and on to maternal influence.
Those silent Sisters of the dale
still muted in their reverence.

A thoroughfare. Two turns
take me toward Tormore
and Nan. Like wildfire she burns
these bushes. Her ever open door...

And so I leave this tar behind,
to head north. Older wheels
carry us to the homes we mind,
at least, that's how it feels.

Teach an Cheoil

(The Music house)

for all the young musicians

Musically speaking, the lilting whispers beyond
are discordant. But these tunes in rooms
are full of learning. Young fingers lift off and on
over and over, one more time. A deadline looms

for the fleadh, the party, for the wee gig.
Such excitement in airs blown through reels
and hornpipes but important they *listen* to the jig,
to the tap on a tile and the uniformity of heels.

Their teachers, with the experience of years
sound out the trickier parts and identify lost notes
in a word. Mums and dads with often untrained ears
look on amazed. They still tie laces, put on coats

but what skills are growing in the breath of a flute,
the shrill of whistles, the draw of a bow,
the crispness of banjos and at the base the astute
taps of a bodhrán. A pulse, deep and low.

And as quickly they are gone to childish cares.
To homeworks, adventures and the days of youth.
The rooms regain themselves and the now silent chairs
appear all the more empty. But in truth

it is a temporary calm, their patience is sound.
We who remain return to our own search, seeking
the harmonies of life which do all surround
the lilting whispers beyond, musically speaking.

Accordion

for Ciarán O'Kane
Attached by leather link,
umbilical, life's security.
Its angle precarious I think
but it breathes with surety

of purpose for they that dare.
Fingers fast, treble and bass,
on buttons or keys taking air
to every conceivable place.

The Irish lung, whose voices
flow from foreign streams
as Soprani meets James Joyce.
To dance in day dreams

with Castagnari or Hohner
in Kerry sets. Spinning round
the houses in their honour...
reel, polka, jig. The sound

of energy, drawn, pushed,
pulled and steered along
octaves. Then all hushed
to cradle some quiet song.

A slide, down a Salterelle,
the steel or wood surround
ornate and does swiftly tell
heels to hit the ground.

Variety in its shape and rows,
but constant its allure,
scribing its melodic prose
from Gaelic wells, deep. Pure.

Christmas (bel1)eve

Around cribs flame thoughts gain brightness.
Their glow fuelled in reminiscence and recall
of December's curious contrast, her kindness
in spite of sleet and snow, storm and squall.

Such inclemency, mirrored in behaviour,
is overcome in what good will remains
and the birth of a child some call saviour.
For others their children bring similar gains.

But either or both, if your heart's invested
generosity of spirit is fair consequence.
Where faith is strong truth can't be contested
by minds debating all innocence

captured in youngsters, wondering and waiting
'neath elfish eyes that would spill the beans.
All actions noted, imaginations salivating
at the promise of magic. The demands of teens,

now wholly involved in our festive charade.
Children, but a childish layer they've shed
and in that one might pause, even feel sad.
But no, our master stroke is soon to be played.

Long lists, long gone in longing looks at fires,
the smoke the dream deliverer as bed beckons.
Tomorrow rarely so excites or youth inspires
in its tick to morning, the ecstasy of seconds.

Prepared we look in, sleep has them sound.
I envy their calm, but there is not the will,
or need to complain. Cool wrapped the ground,
for hooves and rooftop steps I listen still.

Doors

In front of us are many doors,
keyed by the eye
and that we have fulfilled our chores
we shall enter by and by.

Doors as these do not have locks
nor or they made of wood
neither are they hard like rocks
that suffer fire and flood.

These are portals to the mind
that patiently await
visits from both fair and kind
through imagination's gate.

For surely you have guessed
these doors are merely covers
to terrific tales tall that test
the bravery of lovers

and the very heart of dreams
that follow swiftly there.
Such plots to find, such schemes
to inflame the very air.

I'll read aloud each magic line
a layer on the last
and notice when his eyes meet mine
the joys of Christmas past.

I smooth my fingers slowly down,
pages white and thin
leading further round and round
the adventure we are in.

We nightly travel many worlds
standing in his room,
and he the captain fire unfurls
in avoidance of our doom.

The doorways we do chance to cross
on excitement hinges
and perfection is our gain, no loss
before tiredness twinges.

Not Fade Away

We see them on our screens running
from an enemy, unseen and cunning.
They are mostly soaked in dust and blood
with children, or some remains. What should
be children but are less, no more.

We see the greyness of a town's destruction,
steel punctured, concrete shelled constructions.
There are plastic pots and colourful clothes
amongst the stones and rubble which propose
a normality that resided here before.

We hear them squeal at loss and death.
Their hands flail, they gasp for a breath
of air to inhale against the annihilation
of life. We imagine their situation
and fail. We can't imagine pain that sore.

We see the doctors, green clad and tired.
Holding babies, consoling parents mired
in the turmoil of bereavement.
They work on amid all, an achievement
shared on each and every floor.

We hear the leaders explain their actions.
'It's the fault of warring factions
upon whom we must deliver fire
and wind. So that they may not aspire
to equality, they shall remain poor.'

We must not believe all that's said
by those who'd reconstitute the dead
as some noble cause; as some thin facade
for genocide. Policies of men made mad
who listen to the truth no more.

Soon enough the next war will end
and calmed by desire to see all mend
we'll turn away. Our attentions shift
to other issues, leaving those unseen to sift
through what horrors lie in store.

Missing in Action

Of all the terms to abuse
heroism, 'missing in action' I'd choose.
Not for the one disappeared.
No, for governments that have cleared

their desks of effort, responsibility.
For the suits who deflect culpability
and blame the victim, the oppressed
who now, with apathy are detested.

They, in all gruesome clarity,
an eyesore. Almost beyond charity
as, in the land of crucifixions,
they embody man's contradictions,

his terror, his terrorism and hate.
For such children it's too late.
Buried firstly, in rubble, delivered
via jet or bomb and slivered

limb from limb. Decapitated.
Prevaricated over, eradicated
in their hundreds. Each one
a daughter and somebody's son.

And secondly, mired in news.
Headlines, that fit western views
and talk of democracy and choice.
What words when your voice

is dust? But we can speak out,
though removed. We can shout
and display against lies and deceit,
where 'feet on the ground' compete

and unite. How shall we explain
when asked by our children again
and again? That in spite of our flaws
we did not live for a cause?

No Offence

It seemed because I was aware
of the world, of news and of reporters
it was history. That somehow we where
beyond all that. Riots, bombs, mortars,

shoot to kill, invasions, miners' strikes.
I'd watch clips from thirty years hence
and think 'I'm glad we don't see the likes
of that these days.' No offence

of course, but that was lesser living.
Nowadays it wouldn't occur, that toxic
waste. We've moved on. We're forgiving,
cultured, wise, healthy, democratic.

How arrogant; or at best naive
was I to expect our primal nature
to be tempered? Why believe
that there would be a calmer future

in years to come? Yes, love exists
and good people mingle and mix
without much rancour. But the twists
of the heart run deeper than any fix

so far attempted. And the evidence
is clear and continues to cloud, to hang
like a sigh and interrupt our sense
of right to the point we've strangled

reason from the horror and justify Hell.
For God and glory, for ground and oil,
for a book of stories that holy men tell.
For skin colours that bubble and boil

in a poison pot we stir and scatter
in half thoughts and occasional phrases.
For stretches of land and water matter
more than you and I which raises

the disturbing truth that we are at war
within. We soldiers of Christianity,
of Islam. We prophets of money and power
define the scars of so called humanity.

When the need for '*why*' him strikes
our son will watch some thirty years hence.
And think 'I'm glad we don't see the likes
of that these days. No offence.'

Playing Dead

On picking up his plastic toy
I thought, My God! What have I done?
Imbuing play for our wee boy
with a thing as vicious as a gun.

Sure it's only sport, they charge around.
No one hurt, their voices pop.
'Til next I thought about the sound
of teasing Hell. My heart did stop.

Ah, little boys, they're all the same?
They fire fake bullets, hit the floor...
But what message this rotten game
that adults mirror more and more?

I wondered at their sense of fun
in shooting although make believe,
and causing death meant to my son
laughter without cause to grieve.

"Won't you teach him good from bad?"
"Won't you say it's wrong to kill?"
I'll tell him too no sense is had
in playing dead for good or ill.

Play Ground

Do they fly too close to the sun? Or perhaps
not close enough? Ankle feathers bring mishaps,

bumps and crashes. Like protons and neurons
such chaotic collisions yield energy. Pile-ons

and red faces, tears, runny noses and scrapes.
Scraps over football, tig, hide and seek, japes

and incessant chat; the noise of young minds
thrown together and free in playground confines.

Superheroes all, flying creatures, battle scars,
illegal aliens and a history of world wars

suggests an origin. Glimpses of bickering,
pulling, tugging and shoving. But their flickering

lights promise much more. Although every day
in over worn shirts that overhang school grey

trousers and skirts, their inner colours are merely
contained a while. The experienced sincerely

hope they find a canvas. Today I walked between
altering my path for those who had not seen

me. They whirled away and dived in laughter
as I, with a few more years, followed slowly after.

But not in regret, I do not envy their fun
Instead my youth again I enjoy in our son

and daughter who have yet to plot or mend
but will, with luck, find all the world a friend.

Thunder and Lightning

At one time I used my tip toes to ring the bell.
The world was big and I was not at all.

My memory is a touch unclear but does tell
me of adventure and excitement. Of being small.

A wee lad, a wee fella, a wee craitur
climbing things and falling off. Crying at the loss

of my team in big matches. Fanatical by nature
prone to tears, when tears were okay and got me 'aws'

But this was a foray. This day I went alone.
No reason but divilment. "Now pick a door.

That'll do. The oul' hag lives there, a no threat zone.
She'll not catch me. Knock it hard, like Thor.

Run like lightning." Too confident I just ran
round the corner. Within earshot of her breath

which came slow but sure. Fell her hand
and caught me. Skulking. Afraid to death

of the consequences which would swiftly come.
But not the ones this child expected.

No, for she smiled. 'Would you like some
chocolate?' A soggy nod as I accepted

a Penguin. Its wrapper slid about my fingers
until I set it free. Then ate it. In two goes.

She bid me leave but in my mind she lingers.
Why did she forgive me? Only she knows.

Evening in September

There is a fatigue in September grass,
the exasperations of seasonal change.
More saffron than anything, the passage
of the sun in echo by time so arranged.

Ragweeds too on the wane, wrestling
with destiny. Their hearts diluted, spent.
They'll hunker down, like the nestling
mosses on river rocks, subtle and unkempt.

In a matted glen late mist meanders
to night. Its visits have momentum
and bully light reducing her splendours
to harbingers of the darkness to come.

And what of the river? The life sound
of energy and calm all combined.
It creeps around stones, as if the ground
would rebel and with sight be entwined.

In some aftermath of effort, these days
offer all, for the fortunate who would see.
With its cool generosity Autumn plays
on heartstrings, music for you and me.

Daylight Saving

I find again I can't dismiss
at different places in my day,
the incremental brightness kiss
that February gives away.

Last evening in a music hour
I walked among the freshly sown
seeds of learning, coming flowers
of younger gardens still ungrown.

At the window whence I stood
the darkness seemed somewhat afraid
and was further back, as if it would
choose Spring itself to be delayed.

The swirl of worlds about the sun
with gravity and tilt and tide,
forces change on everyone
eternal seasons cannot hide.

Winter's hand, the empty husk
clings to trees, to weed and rose
but withers daily now at dusk,
confidence in day light grows.

Tomorrow at some time no doubt
I will see night tides arrive
and every wave will splash about
the footsteps of us all, revived.

Getting Like Thunder

The weight of colour is borne of forest green
and midnight, the bearer of torrents and reminder

of days before the testing of arks was seen.
Moisture bubbles under the skin of once kinder

skies, which now offer the red horizon as a gift,
a promise of better after the ensuing storm.

The late sun's furnace orange serves to lift
coolness and reinvest heat seaward, warm

and lush in such evenings and her comrades.
The kernel of life itself is reflected in drops

festooning every leaf, every flower and blades
too numerous as light fades and slowly stops.

I am almost drowned in air, gorged on potential,
tick full, I bow before the marching clouds

and their import. Soon the silent heavens shall
ripen and split forcing down their many shrouds

of ill at ease elements doomed to battle drench
our edge damp sod for loan heavy tomorrows.

I inhale the nectar of it, arms open, and unclench
my heart. These moments overwhelm many sorrows.

Finger Chase

For Katie

I strain to see but they're beyond sight,
at least, to the eyes of many mornings.
But as sure as dewdrops follow night
they're here, in spite of many warnings

received about the company of men.
As day releases dawn I watch her face,
her gaze, the where and when
of contact. Fingers flow at rhyming pace.

Does she mean to one entrap? To hold?
Marionettes know such rise and fall
onto coloured strings as does unfold
seduction, tones to warm the ears of all.

Their playground some wondrous wood,
curved, symbol of enchanted land.
Its resonance untold but understood
in octaves, taking listeners by the hand.

A grin concludes, the vibrations calm,
we are released unhappily from rapture.
She quick peeks into her empty palm
to reveal just that, no prize, no capture,

except of us. Their game of chase is run
'til on her to call they will decide.
The other world reveals what can be done
when her little friends and she confide.

Flute

For Catherine

What colour is the soul? What would you say
is its hue? How much could it weigh?
What of its texture? Would you imagine it to be
rough, smooth, hard or soft, captured or free?

Theology may answer but I know its sound
and where it resides, waiting to be found.
It is breath and heart, sadness and laughter,
within the flute emotion comes dancing after.

From night honoured blackness, breaks light
and tone centuries designed. But to get it right
requires the solidarity of endurance, the stress
of time, the feel of truth and musical finesse.

The inhale of the gossip, the town crier, mixed
with whispers of bed time when dreams are fixed
and controlled. They temper the wave and tide
of exhalation where intimacy and passion hide.

Such effort and reward combined never more so
than in the slow air of slow airs, sanctuaries of woe
and loss. The wordless here recant their dreams
coldly scattered in the painful octaves of screams.

But sorrow does not hold opinion too long
any more than silence passing by a sad song.
The jig and reel rely on thorough gusts of wind,
the fingers grip and suddenly we are pinned

to the whim of the tunes that come swirling
from the conical artistry and stretched sterling
silver, attached at odd references along its length.
Listen and you will hear Ireland's eternal strength.

Guitar

for Mickey Murphy

Precision she's demanding
from we that would choose
efforts at commanding
variety. The Blues,

Jazz, Gypsy, Rock, Soul
to be found along frets
waiting, veins of gold,
for finger picks. Regrets?

None. Again and again
we enter ever willing
her steel and nylon lanes
to find wells over spilling.

In such depths we divine,
we pan, note by note,
strings all chord enshrined
pressed and held in remote

rooms, earned recollection.
Her sculpted body, curved
in figure eight. The direction
of her neck, open, unreserved.

Her Spanish blood at home
with Irish tunes insistent
in support we do not roam
from rhythms old, consistent

and where myself I find.
Cradled close we prepare
for all songs. My mind
and hands belong to her.

Novices

for Seán Ó Muireagáin
We entered a world of arias,
sounds of the human voice
unmet. What feeling, operas,
intimate passion and choice

beyond normal, (save Luciano,
Nessun Dorma, silk bound prima
donnas). I learned of soprano,
alto, bass, tenor, Papagena,

Papa-papa-papa-Papageno, the layabout,
lover of birds and magic bells.
Harmonies in sea, we drifted out
note rapt, trapped 'neath spells

conjured by courtly magicians.
The intricacy almost too much,
the unity of voice and musicians…
How do they do it? Such

mastery artistic. Of song,
of drama, of music, of movement
all at once? And us swept along
gaining knowledge, improvement.

As quick their rainbow range,
our feast, our spectacle ended
and in our standing the strange
echoes of such beauty befriended

warmed our steps into the night.
We bathed in enchanted dust
and set for home with new sight
and to return? Yes, we must.

Tenor banjo

For Stephen Leech and Paul Conlon
Crisp, like the crackle of fire sticks
her notes snap air. They are the grit
of finer soils, contrast to the soft flicks
embroidered there. No mistaking it.

Her terse tense tones have travelled
far from African cousins across skin
and wood and steel and are unravelled
sharply, picking the company therein.

Who would smooth her rougher edges?
Who would dare to bridle lightning?
I have seen many, cornering on ledges
eyes transfixed and knuckles whitening.

Her parts a motley array, but in time
resonate bones from head to heel.
Execution the key, like metered rhyme
exacting the essence from jig and reel.

Her slender neck waits impatiently
the touch of fleshy palms and fingertips.
Fret fronted and pearl lined frequently,
inlaid the energy of touching lips.

Her notes in triplicate, quadruples,
blaze four wound willing strings…
Her champions will soften her scruples
and enlighten this most modest of things.

The Other Mountain

What care I for socks?
when barefoot on rocks
oblivious to clocks
and a meaningless shirt?
For everyone knows
with a stream on your toes
life itself shows
a way through the dirt.

This innate desire
to push higher and higher
with our feet in the mire,
that scrap yard of souls.
A yearning for stuff
though we've more than enough
and away in a huff
when money's burnt holes.

And old father Time
slips away with each rhyme
yet after each chime
we rush on again.
Faster and faster
we're courting disaster
Mankind with no master
treats the world with disdain.

The sun splits the stones
as reckless young bones
carry their phones
like some holy grail.
The ice says farewell
to where I can't tell
but Poseidon will yell
With high water and gale!

But it's hard for us all
to answer the call
and watch the leaves fall
the way that we should.
There's the making of money,
like hay when it's sunny,
or bees with the honey
If only we could.

Happiness guaranteed?
Each financial need
sorted with speed
how grand would it be?
The pressure would fade
our dreams would be made
to Hell with the spade
of work we'd be free!

But what next my friend?
There's so much you can spend
and at the day's end
you're alone with your wealth.
For the oddities of life
with their troubles and strife
put the edge on each knife
and a value on health.

But there goes the bleeper
The clock is my keeper
time's getting no cheaper
And I must away.
Sure I'll dry off my toes
and as the wind blows
this spot that I chose
I'll revisit some day.

Bird Song?

Above and around, at rest or in flight
over tree tops, on branches, out of sight

I hear birdsong, filtered by leaves.
Robins, house martins altering eaves

so that not only rain drops fall.
Pigeons, thrushes and cuckoos call

our musical ear and bid it listen
to their gift. But all that glistens

as they say and the same is true
of fierce feathered rhapsodies in blue.

Warfare on high, primeval urges,
tail chasing, guttural sex driven dirges

and all to get laid, those eggs.
Strutting on prima donna like legs

the males of the species puffing
their chests, preening and fluffing

for ladies, boudoirs. 'Oh do come in
and yourself brace for some original sin!'

Rivals repelled, chirps pitch peaked
'Hop along, mate'. Threats boldly squeaked

in arboreal arenas that to those below
seem poetic, blissful, bereft of woe.

But whatever the truth, the why, the how
sing birds sweetly, we under stand now.

Away Day

I stepped from family for a time
to a former life, (no kids or wife)
in Donegal with friends of mine.

The potential for some social sport
our common bond and us all fond
of such sojourns, brief and short.

For they provide us resurrections
of conversations on life's occasions,
its twists, turns and reconnections.

Rekindled at that busy door
in Hudi's bar where who you are
finds warm welcomes to explore.

'How's the form? What's the plan?'
Words ushered out with beer, stout
and 'a while since I seen ye man.'

Our common cause, a trusted friend
a stag became, and chase the game
of choice we'd recommend.

This swirling camaraderie
found us tuned, craic consumed,
amid our mad menagerie.

Not one of us was left behind,
all survived as all contrived
to keep an eye and peace of mind.

The clouded sky of aftermath
summed our state but not too late
rays came through to light a path.

Then into worlds we scattered.
Fond farewells 'til wedding bells
united us and all that mattered.

I stepped back from a former life,
to family, my reasons three
for all time...my kids and wife.

Shadow

for mum

If I've heard it once I've heard it my whole life,
"You are your father's son. The living spit.

And all you do, you didn't lick it off a knife
or find it at the back door, divil the bit."

In it lies some truth but by no means all
for as I gaze on this picture *she* is my shadow.

I didn't see it before, nor overly look at the fall
and rise of features but it is obvious now.

'Tis from a sideways point of view, the scene,
where bones are less defined and faces speak
of other influences, other people that have been.

For no doubt her parents' echoes will seek
her out. Through this revelation I now learn

to look more carefully at my own reflection.
To ignore superfluous compliments unearned

in comparisons and continue in my own direction
taking her along as much and more than he.
For her story was forged in the heated trials

of fifty thousand Croke Park voices, a melee
of fervour. In a silent corridor where a boy's smiles

were warmly met by hidden tears and dread
that in spite of all help, worldly and above,

the high likelihood the boy would soon be dead.
She knew no other way but to show him love,

to give. Back to the picture I cast my eyes
not having expected it to so openly show

the other side of me. Only in time do I realise
that she is company no matter where I go.

Picture book

I do not see you anymore, except in pictures,
photographs, that type of thing. You're frozen

there with a smile or some turn of features
and I remember the day, camera chosen.

I do prefer photo albums. Ones that crinkle
and happily yield to angles before turning

a page. Screens do not allow for the sprinkle
of magic found in such nor is the yearning

of quite the same measure. Perhaps it's just me,
clutching for a piece of you in these fading

images, with their imperfections and disparity
of size. Placed in slow order too, not invading

the mind's eye via click or swipe. I savour
them, each one, each morsel of you that I miss.

In black and white, sepia, the warmth and flavour
of tea, a hug at night or good morning kiss.

I hear you in the second that shutter closed
in faux anxiety, not caring to pose just then,

embarrassed maybe. But I love it, for it shows
the reality of you, of us all, away back when.

Something calls me back to life, here, now
and I shall close this treasure trove, this book

of photographs where in my days somehow
an eternal you awaits each time I take a look.

The half house

I stare stranger like on an ancient skill,
thatch. By the thousand, cut insulating straws
trimmed and thick. The ladders long down and still
I hear their tea time voices and confused crows' caws.

To the half door, red and round the back.
No study in grandeur yet fit for kings
and priests, who would smile at its lack
of conformity as turf burns and a kettle sings.

And what a stage! Of black sooted white,
where patient time stained fire rods, pokers and pans
know the applause hungry bog smoke just might
deny the stack and return to less than adoring fans.

Ridged and uneven walls entice the pave stoned floor
to out slant them in a game of fun.
Giggling nooks and crannies keep the steady score
of visiting heads, bumped one by one.

The children's voices fit, snugly in a bunked room.
Their Gaelic petals arouse the memories of stones
to sounds long forgotten but now shining through the gloom
of myths and legendary tales of swords and shields and bones.

But 'tis back to the fireside, smoke bound or not
where music and craic are forged. In such misty heat
yarns and half-truths outweigh honesty at this spot
that finds its way in song and gentle taps of feet.

So it is with relieved reluctance that we now vacate
this slow ticking time-piece for the modern vice
of comfortable things, that our time cannot placate,
wishing to return again to something half as nice.

Curtains

for helen and Roseanne

An involuntary twitch? The curtains moved
as I walked by, as I walked by with my beloved.
And a shadow from behind did shift
as we walked by, enjoying the human gift

of love. 'The wind perhaps. An open door?'
I mused, did wake the curtain, nothing more
as I walked by with her hand in hand.
Until a frowning eye on us did land.

A frowning eye and furrowed brow in silence
roared its disapproval, its non compliance
to our living sin. To the freedom of our choice
that would be stifled in that voice

from the safety of a window, blinded
to we who don't conform nor or minded
by some ancient text. The rule book of behaviour
thrown from half open doors, that says a saviour

will ban us to Hell for our way of life.
Creaks on hinges light the path to strife
and anger. Discrimination because not wed locked
I bore a child, love it and God have mocked.

But no. Not for me the God of shouldn't.
Not for me the God of brimstone who wouldn't
know love if by it he was smote.
That is not the way of faith. Let me just quote

another line from someone real, on this earth,
the man of dreams, who to the world showed his worth
and said 'only love can drive out hate'.
And so, I'll love my neighbour though she will wait

behind the curtain and talk of me, of us.
But we'll greet her proudly and in time thus
will her curtains rest. She I trust will come to see
true love guides both you and me.

Suit

for Mick Quinn R.I.P.

I never feel right in a suit. It restrains me somehow.
Too sharp its angles that on bending, complain
against my skin. It is formality, stale air, not allowing
for breezes. I'd be happy never wearing one again.

But I knew a man. He warm welcomed me at his door
from where I'd listen and learn and be amazed.
He invariably wore a suit: matched in halves, coloured
blue, well cut. On him it was soft; the dusk of days;

the stream among rocks; the yellowness on whins.
Not self importance, it offered wisdom, greeting
in a bar or a room of stories. Scandalous sins
captured in verse. Belly laughs at such meetings

where the likes of his likes held court, held us all.
I always knew about him. Recent summer moments
let me get to know him and I stood in his broad hall.
As quick we'd be at wave length and I got a sense

of time. I reflected in his glasses and saw myself.
Honoured indeed. He has since loosened the tie,
unbuttoned the shirt and hung his cap upon the shelf.
I'll look out for him, I know I'll hear him by and by.

enough

for Mick O'Driscoll

I knew he was somewhere here,
over someplace talking and drinking.
I was there too, close by and near
enough. Near enough to be thinking

how delighted I was. Together
after an interlude of too many days.
And now, like better weather's
implications, our spirits were raised.

That is to say it was enough
that we were mutual harbours.
I turned my back, into the rough
and ready fire of musical hours.

At intervals we'd cross for Stout
and he'd lean in, surveying fields
and gauging furrows and all about.
Orders wordless amongst reels.

We drifted atop intermittent tides
until closing time's solemnity
emptied Coili's swirling insides
and we ventured out in unity.

Confident on my returning road
north, away from Galway west,
that time, events can not erode.
I will visit us when echoes test.

Jetsam

The tide's eternal journey is wave white
and constant. It will melt stone
and reshape the souls of day and night.
Heartbeats slow around flesh and bone

and often we take our children there.
Today on some other shore, the sea
washed to land more than salted air.
Upon the sand I counted twenty three

of various years no more than five.
The age when lives blossom red,
when thoughts come, when they strive
to hold the world as they might bread

or a toy. But here were no voices
nor excitement. Instead soaking hair
moved with the water. Their choices
removed all by war and lying there

those kids in two broke my heart.
Bedraggled, pathetic flotsam cast
to Hell and I am changed in part,
knowing they will not be the last.

The Troubles

We *all* have the 'Troubles', those inner voice bubbles
that shout, shock and bitterly suppress
sunlight. Their resolution? Anyone's guess
but we must or watch lives turn to rubble,

stone by stone. Some solace in groups
to thrash out demons, stab at the heart
of it. The end of Hell? Perhaps the start
of someone new. Send in the troops

for I hear freedom like Martin L King.
Sometimes I too have a dream, whirring
through the night when nothing is stirring
as sleep attends the burn of some thing

in the white heat of silence. Thought fireworks
bang and scream in that mythical calm
of stress and cyclical errors where I am
weak and each concern of modern life lurks.

The 'Troubles'. Not just those labelled
to describe northern friction. The forty year war
fought and still fought to describe what we are,
'Terrorist? 'Victim?'' Only in tales old and fabled

do we play such roles. As if words eased the pain
of what love leaves behind. They quantify loss.
With such cold terms they dictate how this cost
should be paid. And they do so again and again.

We all have the 'Troubles' but here is the twist,
for we all have a voice and with it can share
bits of each other. Those kept away, hidden and rare
and would rather our self examiner missed.

But the sky will not fall upon their disclosure
and only those close will find what is hidden.
Their exhumation no crime, and it is not forbidden
to cry, sob and shake in sympathetic exposure.

Trams

My friend and I travel on trams. Big metal,
slow wheeled, carrying us eternally.
They look almost the same, having settled
in grooves, entrenched. Occasionally

I see these similarities, characteristics
of sameness. Old transports seldom meet
except at junctions, where spotters' statistics
and comments are tallied on main street.

Trams have large windows, breath cleaned,
so that if I want I can look in at my friend.
He can see me too. One day I over leaned
and almost fell out, not that I feared my end

for I was swiftly pulled back, patted down,
scolded and told 'don't be so remiss.'
Many on the tram lean out. Others just frown,
remain seated and do not approve of this

behaviour. Some of the stations en route
are in need of repair. Number twelve is rough.
We hardly speak passing by, the music of flute
and drum speaks plenty and says quite enough.

My friend's tram doesn't care for seventeen.
Some travellers have lodged complaints
about the décor. 'An unapologetic green'
they call it and would rather different paints.

Coming cutbacks mean services are changing.
The number of trams must, they say, reduce.
We will have to, they say, start rearranging
ourselves onto shared lines. I can't deduce

exactly how that will work. We're well used
to our tracks. We know each bump, every turn
of these trundling timepieces that have confused
contact. I might just get off… and learn.

As the Crow Flies

Famously straight lined. That is to say
they do not veer in any direction.

Between two the quickest route today
sees him stare at his own reflection.

Compared to other functional features
his eyes contain white lightning.

It rails against confinement, a creature
caged, all teeth and gut frightening

roar. But his bars are reinforced
with doubt and insecurity's steel.

He glances, seeing their black course
resolve in some freshly cut hay field

just beyond. He closes his eyes,
and turns slow, away from the glass.

He will soon electrify his own skies
and fly directly, over any impasse.

Upon a Laneway Late

Tractor wide the lane we walk, my son and I.
Central grass unshorn, hedges wild, head high
and though the nettles outreach him
and buttercups top his knee,
we are sheltered from the wind
a time, the boy and me.

Stones and twigs underfoot, dirty puddles laze
all tempting youth with last minute swerve aways.
Fence framed rabbits in his sights
see the hunter stalk his prey.
But with little guile, the driven sprite
returns with less to say.

A sleeping silver gate, unopened for a time
acts as barrier to a yard, over it we climb.
The long abandoned house awaits
and now not so far ahead
he turns and coyly negotiates,
"You first." Behind he's sped.

Plaster shy, uneven, stacked blocks converse
in deliberate lines and window glass is scarce
but for stubborn shards edge long.
Hand gripped, eyes moon bright
on seeing a dead rook, once strong
and loud, now quieter than night.

On a broken flight of stairs the flightless crow
is avoided with all the length a step can know.
We peer onto a second floor
and rooms vague in definition.
He peers harder on an old front door
"Time to go," his requisition.

He discovers curiosity, cunning, even fear
splash similar shores. Maybe in another year
he'll return, imagination ready.
He rides at pace along the lane,
I follow into dusk all steady
the desire we take such walks again.

Ór (Gold)

We speak in tongues. Our rhythms different, our sounds
from untamed regions of the throat. At least to our ears.

In the confusion and curiosity we seek middle ground,
an area of beginning. English language for so many years

> the currency of status and power is our compromise.
> But it is not enough for him. English but the tool,

> the lump hammer and chisel to find what really lies
> under our skin. For lifetimes Irish portrayed as fool

> and foolish is now his ambition. He yearns its mystery
> and we having allowed its return have become hosts

> and guardians, teachers and retellers of a new history.
> At Glencolmkille to learn and now on other coasts

> he enters a living lesson. But this is not our whim.
> Nor is it some dainty affectation for foreign intrigue.

It is us. Our lives lived in original vowels which to him
are sustenance and validation. He is refreshed, fatigue

> defeated. He begins again in the sounds of rivers,
> the rhythm of hedges and grass, the tonal inclination

> of clouds and rain. His pride in it, the sun. Shivers
> run through me. Our daughter cements the occasion

> and offers greeting. The future of it away to some tree,
> to climb, healthy and adventurous. He is content

> and with miles to go moves on in a kind of liberty.
> The Irish journey is what his efforts represent.

big bike

"Are you ready?" I ask. He nods in haste.
"Good man," I reply, holding the seat.
We push off unsteady at walking pace.

My fingers circle the grip, hiding his hand,
in control. The set up complete
I increase speed and feel him take command

of momentum. We miss a blue dinosaur
but fatally alter an unwary snail.
The full washing line billows out toward

us. "Plough on," I shout. He drives down
the pedal. Made it! Next, our trail
leads us to fresh cut grass. I steer around

buttercups and we decapitate daisies.
He is pulling away, nearly free.
"Hold me. Dad!" But I don't. Amazed

he sees my hands, off the handle bar.
He's caught between fear and liberty
and it almost ends. I am now too far

behind for rescue. His time has come,
his face alive with life, he thrives
in the solidarity. Faster, into some

new era he rides his big bike, the one
he had to grow into. High fives
and hugs on landing. "Fair play son."

Splash

That we could soak you in new memories;
hold you aloft and layer you in laughter,
friendship, fun and shortly after
thick cover you in joy like pizza cheese.

That we could make such moments heat white
and sear them deep, ready to call upon.
So quickly they arrive but soon are gone
into the evening mist, sunset and night.

That we could bottle such seconds, so distilled
by excitement and frenetic abandon.
We'd offer them when thirst's dry hand on
your shoulder rests and see you rebuild.

That we could surround you by musical moat
and see you leap in, splash, then swim
about in tunes and at your whim
use all their rhythms to keep you afloat.

That we could picture you now as life planned;
honouring freedom, worshipping youth
reminding you (when longer in the tooth)
of happiness. THAT, we can.

Name

I have no people in this graveyard
nor am I familiar with the names
engraved. Undefined plots and hard
stone slabs, raised slate frames

shape the abundant trimmed grass.
It defers to ritual and repetition
as do we, attendees en masse.
Feelings of sorrow and contrition

are at odds with a sense of place
for here I have none. I recall
other such days in the old spaces
of Saval, Mayobridge, Newry all

interred amid familiar hedgerows.
I knew those vein marbled lines
and letters but my present outgrows
that past. I draw from different mines.

I have no people in this graveyard
but my name will in time appear
as someone new, 'til time's reward
suggests I always was from here.

The Hunt for the Rat

A True Story
For Hugh and Mo

It was 2.15 in the a.m. and dawn a long way away
When Hughie rapped on my door and this to me he did say
"Micheál I reckon I have him, cornered behind the spoon drawer
I need you to block his exit and together we'll vanquish the cur."

A quick rub I gave to the eyelids and donned an oul pair of jeans
Another run out for the t-shirt I was now well set for the scene
I left my sleeping chamber followed Hughie into the hall
Dandered through to the kitchen where this ancient enemy would fall

Our foe was exquisitely cunning the same as the rest of his kind
Small, hairy and vicious and a pest since someone called time
His position was soon established now for the clash of wills
I'd head him off at the pass as Hughie went in for the kill

Above the spot where he crouched was a worktop a little bit loose
And we slipped it back a fraction to see if the divil had moved
He must have thought it was freedom as light invaded his hide
Cos he made a bound for glory but we timed our closure just right

His tail had surely betrayed him for it lay between worktop and wall
"Look quick now," says Hughie, I did but saw bugger all
The worktop again was shifted, the tail fell as if cut by a blade
Not a sign or smell of the owner who wouldn't be the slightest bit pleased

A small hole was enough for the terror to elude us now he had fled
"FECK," snapped Hugh (an acceptable curse, thanks to the late Fr Ted).
I offered a similar expletive that more suited our obvious bad luck
But all this frothy ill wind did nothing to further our hunt

"Right," says Hughie thinking, "he's in among the saucers and cups."
Says I "If we ever get him, Mo'll be a month washing up!"
Cupboard by cupboard was the plan all would have to be cleared
Says Hugh "If he's under the sink we'll be hokin' about for a year!"

To his hunkers Hugh slowly descended and opened door number one
And I stood armed with a Hurley stick in case he decided to run
No immediate chance for glory so Hughie stripped the top shelf
The bottom was nearly naked, "Jayz where'd we get all the delph?!"

Two more to go including the sink and tension now starting to mount
"Knuckle yer trig," says Hughie ,"strike hard and make it count."
Door two quickly whisked open I yelled "Rebollyeaylye"
"Again no sign of our friend, "I doubt he's away to Australia."

Cup by cup was extracted and saucers laid onto the floor
Like picking glass from a cut 'til now only one piece more
The turn of a pipe in the corner, grey plastic at 90 degrees
Hughie moved it a fraction, out he came, Hugh was quick off his knees

Hugging the wood with his body he went right past Hughie's first strike
The Hurley nipped my right shoulder, "It's us or him the night!"
A metre a second he covered I had adrenalin enough for a bear
Down went my blow with the hurl of course I caught nothing but air

Then hard callous welts and vibrations I felt when my body was still
A shock of electric proportions I thought of Peter Sands on the Hill
On he fled round the skirting a bounding, hairy wee blur
Leapt over three bottles toward me I let out a terrible roar

Amid the throes of the drama a calmness then settled our show
Doors all closed, no escape routes, our boy had nowhere to go
He darted left toward Hughie who smiled and lifted his foot
The rat then made his last squeak under a size 9 Wellington boot

Such sighs of relief and contentment, victory indeed was ours
We shook hands and breathed very deeply, time was right for a Powers
Two healthy gulps then retirement like warriors with BrianBorú
Oh, if you do have a rat in your kitchen, **DON'T** call myself or Hugh!

Also by Michael Sands

Away with Words,

A book of poems of family, home, place and music in North Antrim.

> "What a joy it has been to have discovered this marvellous collection. It represents a bright shaft of welcome sunlight in a wearying world. It is full of joy, hope, intellect and a deep understanding of who we are and the unquestioned importance of hearth, home and music."
>
> Mickey MacConnell, songwriter and journalist

Nut Hollow, The Knife and Nefairious

An epic Irish fantasy adventure set along the magical North Antrim Coast. It tells the tale of the fairies of Nut Hollow, an idyllic spot at the foot of the field where the river runs. They have lived happily these many years but all of a sudden worry knocks upon their doors. Nefairious, the fairy gone bad is back. He plans to claim Nut Hollow as his own and release his dastardly father, Neroh from captivity in the Fairy Thorn. Into this fairy war are thrown two little human girls, who are down at the foot of the field looking for an adventure. Little did they know that an adventure was looking for them!

What the readers have said:

Nicely written and a great read. Would make a great present to stimulate young imaginations even if you are not so young!! Liked it alot and am looking forward to the sequel. – Seanie

Amazingly well written. Such a fun, magical story for children and adults alike. Read this with my son and we both loved it! – Belfast Girl

Clachan's 'Historic Irish Journeys' series

Travels In Ireland - J.G. Kohl
German visitor's of his tour around Ireland before the Great Famine.
Disturbed Ireland – 1881 - Bernard Becker
Letters written as the author travelled around the West of Ireland, visiting key places in the 'Land War'. We meet Captain Boycott.
A Journey throughout Ireland, During the Spring, Summer and Autumn of 1834 - Henry D. Inglis
Inglis travels Ireland attempting to answer the question, 'is Ireland and improving country?'.
The West Of Ireland: Its Existing Condition and Prospects - Henry Coulter
Letters from Saunders's News-Letter relating to the West of Ireland after the partial failure of the harvests of the early 1860s.
Highways and Byways in Donegal and Antrim - Stephen Gwynn
An account of a bike journey written at the end of the 19th Century around Donegal and the Glens of Antrim.

* * * * *

Clachan 'Local History' Series

Henry Coulter's account has been sub-divided into:
The West Of Ireland: Its Existing Condition and Prospects, Part 1, by Henry Coulter. Athlone, Co. Clare and Co. Galway.
The West Of Ireland: Its Existing Condition and Prospects, Part 2, by Henry Coulter. Co. Mayo.
The West Of Ireland: Its Existing Condition and Prospects, Part 3, by Henry Coulter. Cos. Sligo, Donegal, Leitrim and Roscommon.

* * * * *

J.G.Kohl's account has been sub-divided into:.
Travels in Ireland – Part 1, Edgeworthtown, The Shannon, Limerick, Edenvale, Kilrush and Father Mathew.
Travels in Ireland – Part 2, Tarbet, Tralee, Killarney, Bantry, Cork, Kilkenny and Waterford.
Travels in Ireland – Part 3, Wexford, Enniscorthy, Avoca, Glendalough and Dublin.
Travels In Ireland - Part 4 –Dundalk, Newry, Belfast, The Antrim Coast, Rathlin, The Giant's Causeway.

Henry D. Inglis' account has also been sub-divided into:
A Journey throughout Ireland, During the Spring, Summer and Autumn of 1834, Part Dublin, Waterford and Cork.
A Journey throughout Ireland, During the Spring, Summer and Autumn of 1834, Part 2 Kerry, Clare, Limerick and the Shannon and concludes in Athlone.

* * * * *

Stephen Gwynn's account has also been sub-divided into:
Highways and Byways in Donegal and Antrim Part One: Donegal
Highways and Byways in Donegal and Antrim Part: Two - Derry & Co. Antrim

* * * * *

Aghaidh Achadh Mór, The Face of Aghamore – edited by Joe Byrne.
Of enduring interest to local historians and to those with ancestral roots in East Mayo.
Lough Corrib, Its Shores and Islands: with Notices of Lough Mask - by William R. Wilde, Published in 1867. 'A work intended to rescue from oblivion … some of the historic monuments of the country'.
A Statistical and Agricultural Survey of the Co. of Galway – by Hely Dutton
A detailed description of the agricultural conditions and practices of Galway in the early Nineteenth Century.
A History of Sligo: Town and Country, Vol. I, by Terrence O'Rorke
First published in 1889, it remains a work of fascination for anyone with connections to Sligo, and is an important reference for anyone interested in the history of Ireland.
A Step Up – by Pat Nolan
This is the story of the one of the great Irish fishing vessels, the BIM 56-footers.

* * * * *

Poems, Ballads and Songs
Songs of the Glens of Antrim, Moiré O'Neill
Written by a Glenswoman in the dialect of the Glens, and chiefly for the pleasure of other Glens-people.

Clachan Publishing
Clachan Publishing, Ballycastle, Glens of Antrim.

www.ingramcontent.com/pod-product-compliance
Lightning Source LLC
LaVergne TN
LVHW022112080426
835511LV00007B/774